Mallie,

Dream big and when you
do make sure you put a plan
together to make it come true. It's
okay to have feelings and share them with
those you love.

♡ Deanna
Brown, ma, LMHC

To my professor Rene Cox. You are an amazing teacher and therapist. Thanks for believing in me. To my son Gabriel, I think of you daily; you are missed, and I can still remember your infectious smile. Thank you for teaching me about unconditional love and the importance of helping others. My niece Nayasheh I'm so proud of who you are and how you've become a great mother. It has been an honor to watch Aila and E.J. grow into amazing humans that will soon go out into the world and make it a little better. I wouldn't be where I am today without my amazing friends; Teresa, Mary, Arlene, Sandy, Griz, Carol, Kathy, Jessica, and Andrea. To my aunts, Bobby Jo, and Shirley, who are my role models, acting mother figures, cheerleaders, confidants, advisors, and my best encouragers, I love you. Finally, to my husband Eric who makes me believe I can conquer the world with one hand when he is holding the other. This book is for you.

"I'm in a mood today," I say. My mom said I was going to meet someone new.

I can't think, my head hurts, and I'm too tired to be out and about. After all I said I don't want to play especially not today."

"Mom, can't you see I don't want to come here to this office? This will not help me."

She said softly, "You have been feeling blue and I don't know why or what else I can do. So, I brought you here today to work out what is going on in your head and why you stay in bed."

"But mom, I told you, I don't wanna meet anyone, I mean no one, not today and especially not someone new. I just want to go home to my warm bed and forget this was ever said."

"Oh, how many times must I say, Mom, today is not a very good day!"

"My dear Jay, this person you will like. She is here just for you to see."

"No mom please, just let me be."

"I've tried to ask how you are feeling without any luck because you won't say. Perhaps together with her you will find another way. Talking about feelings can be hard there is no doubt. Other children and even adults come to therapy to learn a new route. My hope for you, is that you too can learn new ways to be less and less blue."

"Can't you see my dear, I care, and we will find a way to get you through this awful day. I want to see you smile even if it is just for a while. I don't like to see you blue. So please give her a chance and you will see, talking about your feelings will help. Oh, please, won't you just stay, and see with me?"

I nod my head and reply, "Ooookay."

"Hello, my name is Mary, and I am a therapist. Do you know what a therapist is or what we do?"

"Hi, I'm Jay." He shrugs his shoulders, shakes his head and says, "No. My mom says you help people who feel blue talk about their feelings and learn new ways to feel better in their heads to."

"Why yes, that is true. In my office we will play and talk about your feelings and how best I can help you."

"My sister would like your office. She loves to play in the sandbox outside with me." I put hand on my stomach in hopes my therapist would not see. But despite all of my might my tummy began to rumble and tumble, and my therapist could tell even though I tried to be oh so humble.

Mary said, "Can you feel a rumble in your tummy? How often do you feel this way?" I nodded my head and replied, "Why yes, you see, it happens several times a day."

The therapist said, "When you feel this way it can be helpful to use these puppets and talk about what is in your head."

Jay replied, "The Dinosaur feels sad a lot and could use some tea for his tummy. Could you please help me pour the tea? When we are playing with our dog Bella, she always jumps all over me."

Mary the therapist replied, "Yes, thank you for inviting me to play and for using such kind words like please. What makes you sad Dinosaur?"

Jay replied, "I'm afraid I've been very very bad."

Mary replies, "What makes you think you've been bad?"

Jay replied, "Because my parents fight a lot and look oh so sad."

Mary replied, "Sometimes parents fight this is true, but you haven't done anything wrong to feel bad. It's okay to feel blue and we can talk more about how this impacts you."

"But I'm afraid they will break up and there is nothing I can do. I know this is why they wanted me to come here to see you."

"When you feel worried or upset, try taking a few deep breaths. Just like this one....two....three...."

I took a deep breath in and then blew it out. I repeated two more times and said, "I can see how breathing can be helpful for me as I counted one…..two…..three…."

"Our dog Bella likes to lick a lot. She can tell when I am down because she comes and sits next to me even when my mom and sister are around. She checks on me if I get up to go away. Bella, doesn't like me to sit in my room because she always wants me to run and play."

Mary said, "Your dog must really love you and she also does not want to see you blue."

Jay replied, "Why yes, I guess this is true."

"See this is me and that one is you."

The therapist said, "I love your drawing. Can you tell me more about what you have drawn here?"

I replied, "Um this is me and I am smiling next to you. In my picture I am happy and for some reason, I do not feel blue."

"Drawing is a good way to express yourself when you find you are feeling down."

I replied, "I like to draw and I'm starting to see even my tummy is not rumbling and tumbling like before. So maybe you really can help me."

Mary replied, "I am so glad to hear that. How would you feel about coming again to see me?"

I nodded my head and replied, "Oh yes, when can this be?"

Mary replied, "I will talk to your mom and see what day she might be free."

"Well, how did it go?" Asked Mom.

"I told you I didn't wanna meet anyone and especially not someone new. I wanted to go home to my bed and to forget all that was swirling around in my poor head."

"I guess now that I've met her, she really isn't someone new. So, I suppose we can return because well, there's much more fun things she says we can do. She helped me talk about my feelings. Which at first, I admit, I did not want to do."

"But once we got started it made me feel less and less blue. I think I am ready to start to talk about my feelings because I see that I am missing out without a doubt."

"I know I have more stuff to learn that might help me with all the swirling, twisting, and twirling in my head. Thankfully she says she has many more toys and games to play and having fun with her helped even helped my tummy not rumble and tumble during my stay. She has helped me see that in time, with her help my blues can go away. Mom, seeing her has made me smile. I didn't think I would feel better, but now I can see, talking about my feelings truly can be useful to me."

Mom replied, "This is great news. I don't like to see you mope and seeing the therapist today has really given our family so much more hope."

The End!

Resource Page

www.Checkpoint.org
Global Mental Health Resources offering 24/7 crisis support and
suicide prevention services for families.

www.nami.org
800-950-NAMI (6264) or info@nami.org · Crisis Text Line – Text
NAMI to 6264
is a National Alliance on Mental Illness with additional resources and
information.

www.Psychologytoday.com
A website to search for therapists in the United States that accepts
insurance or self-pay depending on your preferences. The website lists
the providers experiences in their bio with a picture of the
professional to view prior to the first session.